Electromagnetism at Work

Electromagnetic cranes can be used to lift and move shipping containers onto trucks and ships. The electromagnet is turned on to lift the container. It is turned off to put the container in the required place.

Electricity

Many people think Benjamin Franklin discovered electricity, but by the 1700s, the discovery was thousands of years old.

Ancient Greeks knew electricity was a type of energy. They also knew its energy could transfer from item to item. They learned this by rubbing pieces of fur on amber. They found the fur was drawn to the stone. This is now called **static electricity**, but it didn't have a name back then.

So what did Franklin study? Lightning. He thought lightning was a type of static electricity. To test this, he needed to capture the energy in the air and transfer the charge to something else. So he tied a key to a kite and used a wire to connect the key to a jar that would store the energy. The kite was carried up to the clouds.

Benjamin Franklin

Static at Play

You can create static electricity. Blow up a balloon, rub it against your shirt, and hold it up to a wall. What happens when you let go?

January 9 is National Static Electricity Day in the United States!

Now all Franklin needed was a storm. When the time came, he and his son set up the kite, and then they waited. But Franklin didn't want to wait in the rain, so he took a seat in the barn, where he kept warm and dry. Time passed and he had nearly given up. But then, he noticed the fibers of the string were standing up. Franklin touched the key and he got a jolt.

Franklin was right! There was static electricity in the air. This meant that lightning was electric. But he almost didn't live to tell about his find. Like metal wire, water is a **conductor**. It helps electric charges travel. That means electricity from lightning can travel down a wet string. A man holding that wet string would get quite a jolt. But luckily Franklin did not get struck by lightning.

Even after Franklin's experiment, people knew very little about electricity. It wasn't until later that people found ways to use and control it.

wet lamp

A Bright Idea

The wet lamp uses water's conductivity to create electricity. It turns on and becomes brighter as a thin metal rod slides into the water. To turn the lamp off, the rod is pulled out of the water.

Electricity can be dangerous. Always find an adult to help you with any electrical work you do!

Atoms

The first step to controlling a natural force is understanding it. So what makes electricity work? Science didn't find the answer until the 1800s. That's when scientists discovered the **electron**.

Electrons are very, very small. They are found inside tiny bits of matter called **atoms**. Atoms are also very small. They're much smaller than the tiny cells that make up our bodies! In fact, trillions of atoms fit inside the period at the end of this sentence. We're made up of atoms. So are our friends and pets. Our homes and schools are, too. Even stars are made of atoms. All matter is made of atoms.

Protons are found at the center of atoms. They have a positive charge. Electrons zip around them. They have a negative charge. These two opposites attract. As a result, protons keep electrons in **orbit**. It's a bit like the way the moon orbits Earth.

Every year, your body replaces 98 percent of its atoms.

Atom Model

The atom model below helps scientists visualize atoms. But no one has actually seen one with his or her own eyes. Even the most powerful microscopes only give the general idea of what an atom looks like.

electron

proton

neutron

Atoms also have **neutrons**. They aren't positive or negative. They are neutral. In other words, they are balanced and have no charge. They are found with the protons at the center of an atom. The center of the atom is called the *nucleus*.

A neutral atom has an equal number of protons and electrons. But atoms gain and lose electrons. That makes atoms positive or negative. Atoms seek balance. When positive, they attract electrons. When negative, they push them away.

Electricity is the energy produced by electrons in motion. First, a negative atom sheds an electron. That lost electron jumps to the next atom. The new atom sheds an electron. The cycle continues on and on. The result is a flow of energy.

neutron

electron

nucleus

proton

Protons and neutrons can be broken down into smaller particles called quarks.

Far Out!

If you rub a balloon against your hair, your hair will stand up. That's because electrons have jumped from your hair to the balloon. And the positively charged atoms (+) in your hair are repelled, or pushed away, by each other. So each strand of hair spreads away from the other strands. But the positively charged atoms in your hair are attracted to the negatively charged atoms of the balloon.

– negatively charged atom
+ positively charged atom

Currents and Circuits

The flow of electricity is called a **current**. It comes in two forms: alternating current (AC) and direct current (DC). When we plug in a device at home, it uses AC. In this form, electrons flow from positive to negative, as well as from negative to positive. They alternate between directions. And they travel at very fast speeds!

When batteries power an item, the electrons only flow in one direction. Have you ever noticed the symbols on a battery? They indicate a negative end (-) and a positive end (+). In DC, the flow always starts at the negative end and travels to the positive end.

Electricity flows from a battery when it joins with another object to form a **circuit**. A circuit is like a loop. If a circuit is broken, the flow stops. What happens when you flip down a light switch? The lights turn off because the circuit is broken.

Direct Current

Electric Lemonade

Squeezing a lemon is one way to make lemonade. Here's another way to make some "juice."

1. Find an adult to help you bend copper wire and a paper clip into a U-shape.
2. Roll a lemon to loosen its juices, and then stick in all the sharp ends of the wires.
3. Touch your tongue to both wires. Feel the power of a lemon battery!

The electrical current in our ears sparks the nerves in our brain. This allows us to hear things.

There are two basic types of circuits: series and parallel.

What usually causes a string of lights to go out? One bad bulb. Those lights are in a series circuit. One wire passes through each bulb on the way to the next. If a bulb gets loose or burns out, the circuit breaks. None of the lights will work.

What would happen if all the lights in your home were wired in a series? If a bulb burned out, everything would go dark and stop working. And you wouldn't know which bulb to replace. You would have to check every single light to fix the problem.

It's no surprise that most items in our homes don't use series circuits. Instead, they have parallel circuits. For this type of circuit, each item that needs power has its own separate pathway. The current takes more than one path at the same time. If one path is broken, the others still have juice.

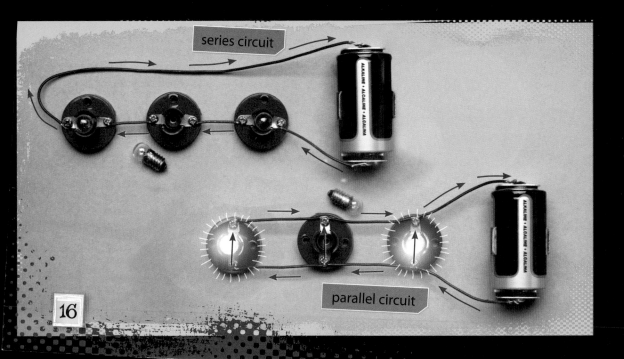

series circuit

parallel circuit

The Power of Measurement

Wattage is the amount of current needed to get a device to work—the higher the wattage, the brighter the lightbulb.

Live Wire

Normally, power lines are safe. But it's important to be careful if they fall. When a line touches the ground, a circuit is created between the downed line and the ground. A person could get an electric shock by standing within that circuit.

Magnetism

Some magnets are formed naturally. One such magnet was found thousands of years ago. It's a rock called *lodestone*.

But most magnets today are made from iron and steel. These materials aren't natural magnets. We train them to be magnets.

Most magnets are made by an electric current. When electrons move in the same direction, they create a current. This makes a magnetic effect. Magnetic objects can attract iron and other metals. But magnets don't attract all metals. Even the strongest magnet can't pick up silver or gold. And nonmetals, such as glass, plastic, and wood, are never attracted to magnets. In gold, plastic, and wood, electrons move in many directions. There is no magnetism.

lodestone

Objects can be magnetized. They can be demagnetized, too. You can change a magnet into a nonmagnet. Just stop the electrons from moving in the same direction.

Training a Magnet

You can easily train a needle to become a magnet. Stroke the end of a sewing needle against one end of a bar magnet for a minute. This sets all the electrons moving in the same direction.

A Sixth Sense

Humans can't feel magnetism. But animals such as sharks, pigeons, and bees can sense it. They use magnetism to find their way.

19

Every magnet has two poles. One is found at each end of a magnet. They're named *north* and *south*, just like the poles on Earth. Opposite poles attract. The north and south poles draw each other near. But two like poles repel each other. For example, two north poles will push each other away.

Every magnet has a limit to its force. The area it can affect is its *magnetic field*. Fields are areas where forces influence objects. The stronger the magnet is, the bigger its field will be. But bigger doesn't always mean stronger. The strongest magnet on Earth is 500,000 times stronger than the biggest one. Can you guess what the biggest magnet is? Earth itself!

Field lines come together at the magnetic poles. This is where magnetic force is strongest.

Planet Magnet

Scientists think Earth acts as a magnet because its core is mostly hot, liquid iron. As Earth spins, a magnetic force is produced.

Electromagnetism

Scientists found the link between electricity and magnetism almost 200 years ago.

Hans Christian Oersted (UR-sted) noted it first. He was showing friends how metal acts as a conductor. That's when he saw his compass needle move. Oersted knew right away he found a link between electricity and magnetism. But he couldn't figure out how and why it worked.

Today, scientists understand magnets much more deeply. They've found ways to create electromagnets, which are much stronger than regular magnets. And they're everywhere you turn. All electric motors use them. They are what make motors spin. They start our cars and help us mow our lawns. They even make our fans work. An electromagnet is at the heart of every power plant. It creates energy inside a **generator**. That's how electricity gets to our homes. Every speaker uses them. Your radio, MP3 dock, and headphones have them inside. So do phones, TVs, and computers. They're even at the amusement park. There, they speed up and slow down the fastest rides.

Types of Magnets

magnetite

Natural

- found in the ground
- always on

Temporary

- man-made
- created by stroking an object with a permanent magnet
- lose their magnetism over time or when dropped or heated

Permanent

- man-made, hold their magnetism
- usually made of iron
- always on

Electromagnet

- iron or steel inside a **coiled** wire connected to an electric current
- stronger than ordinary magnets
- can be turned on and off

Electricity creates a magnetic field. But a moving magnet also creates an electric field! That means you can create a magnet using electricity. And you can create electricity using a magnet. This process is called **induction**.

Wires are thin, flexible pieces of metal. They are often used in electrical work. Usually in a wire, electrons move in all directions. When a magnetic field moves across the wire, the electrons suddenly travel in the same direction. That creates a current. The current can be weak or strong depending on the strength and speed of the magnetic field. If the wire is coiled, so the magnetic field passes through several lengths of wire, more electrons will be affected. That makes the current stronger, too.

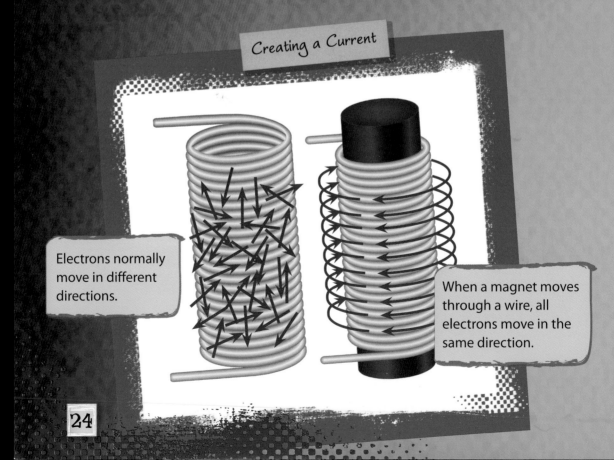

Creating a Current

Electrons normally move in different directions.

When a magnet moves through a wire, all electrons move in the same direction.

Induction in Action

Magnetic fields can be used to induce current in some bicycle headlights. As the bicycle moves, the tire turns a wheel on top of a small container holding a magnet. This turns a magnet inside. A current is induced. The current travels through the wire. It powers the lamp on the bicycle.

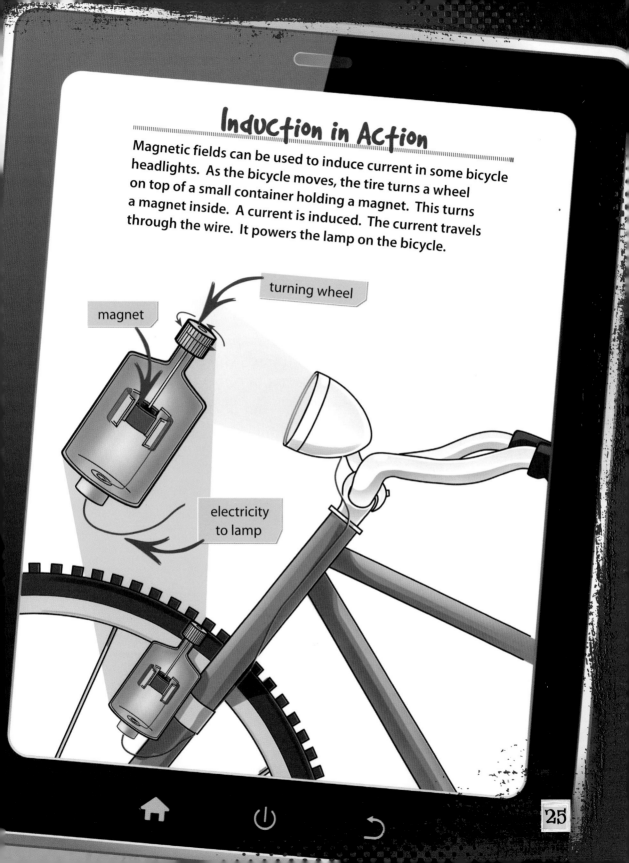

turning wheel

magnet

electricity to lamp

Knowledge Is Power

We're still exploring all that electromagnetic force can do. New, super-fast trains now use electromagnetic rails. They float above the track. NASA is creating a new launch system with electromagnets. It will carry a jet across a runway at a speed of 390 kilometers per hour (240 miles per hour)!

Electromagnetism is creating the future. But it's also a force we already use every day. It powers the world as we know it. It's at work when your alarm clock goes off. And it's there when you get out of bed to turn on the lights. It's with you when you ride in a car or a bus to school. And it allows you to listen to music or watch TV when you return home.

You may not have known its name. But by now it's clear— knowledge of electromagnetism is power!

Electromagnetic force is extremely strong. It's even stronger than gravity!

Think Like a Scientist

What does it take to build a magnet?
Experiment and find out!

What to Get

- 9-volt battery
- insulated copper wire
- metal paper clips
- pencil or large nail

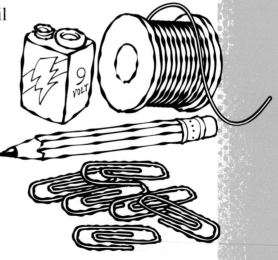

What to Do

1 Wrap the wire in a coil around the pencil or large nail. Leave a few inches of copper wire loose at each end. (Have an adult clip the wire if it is too long.)

2 Wrap each of the loose parts of the wire around one of the two battery terminals. (The terminal is the part that sticks up above the main shape.)

3 Hold your electromagnet over a pile of paper clips. Observe what happens.

4 Experiment with the magnet's strength. Repeat the experiment. Each time, make the coils looser or tighter. What difference does the change make? Record your results in a table like the one below.
*Note:** When finished, disconnect wire from battery to avoid overheating.

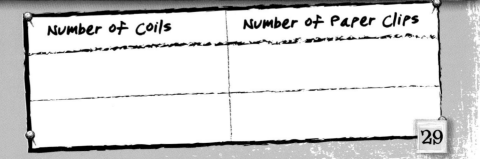

Number of Coils	Number of Paper Clips

Glossary

atoms—tiny particles that make up all matter

circuit—the complete path that an electric current travels along

coiled—wound into circles

conductor—a material or object that allows electricity or heat to move through it

current—a flow of electricity

electricity—a form of energy made up of a stream of electrons

electron—a particle that has a negative charge and travels around the nucleus of an atom

generator—a machine that produces electricity

induction—the process by which an electric current, an electric charge, or magnetism is produced in objects by being close to an electric or magnetic field

neutrons—particles with neutral charges and are part of the nucleus of the atom

orbit—the circular path an object follows as it goes around something else

protons—particles that have positive charges and are part of the nucleus of the atom

static electricity—an electrical charge that collects on the surface of things instead of flowing as a current

Index

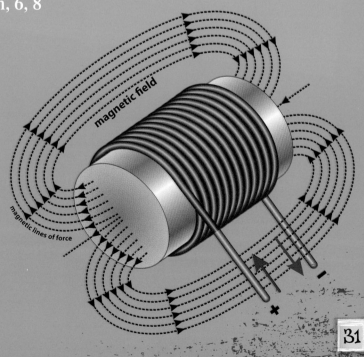

magnetic field

magnetic lines of force

Your Turn!

The Electric Slide

Gather a bunch of friends together. Give each friend an index card with the word *positive* or *negative* written on it. Tape it to the front of each person's shirt. Now, create a dance based on the charges. Remember, opposites attract and like charges repel!